The Homestead Act and Westward Expansion

Settling the Western Frontier

Irene Harris

press™

NEW YORK

Published in 2017 by The Rosen Publishing Group, Inc.
29 East 21st Street, New York, NY 10010

Book Design: Tanya Dellaccio

Photo Credits: Cover Transcendental Graphics/Contributor/Getty Images; p. 4 I. Pilon/Shutterstock.com; pp. 5, 7(left), 7(right), 15 Everett Historical/Shutterstock.com; p. 6 https://commons.wikimedia.org/wiki/File:Louisiana_Purchase.png; p. 8 https://commons.wikimedia.org/wiki/File:Battle_of_Churubusco2.jpg; p. 9 https://en.wikipedia.org/wiki/Treaty_of_Guadalupe_Hidalgo#/media/File:TreatyOfGuadalupeHidalgoCover.jpg; p. 11 https://commons.wikimedia.org/wiki/File:Miners_in_the_Sierras.jpg; p. 12 https://en.wikipedia.org/wiki/Oregon_Trail#/media/File:Alfred_Jacob_Miller_-_Breaking_up_Camp_at_Sunrise_-_Walters_371940142.jpg; p. 13 https://en.wikipedia.org/wiki/Oregon_Trail#/media/File:Bierstadt_Albert_Oregon_Trail.jpg; pp. 14, 18, 20, 21 Courtesy of Library Of Congress; p. 17 https://en.wikipedia.org/wiki/Henry_Clay#/media/File:Henry_Clay.jpg; p. 19 Courtesy of the National Archives.

Library of Congress Cataloging-in-Publication Data

Names: Harris, Irene, author.
Title: The Homestead Act and Westward Expansion : Settling the Western
  Frontier / Irene Harris.
Description: New York : PowerKids Press, 2016. | Series: Spotlight on
  American history | Includes index.
Identifiers: LCCN 2015048097 | ISBN 9781508149576 (pbk.) | ISBN 9781508149439 (library bound) | ISBN 9781508149224 (6 pack)
Subjects: LCSH: Frontier and pioneer life--West (U.S.)--Juvenile literature.
  | Homestead law--West (U.S.)--History--19th century--Juvenile literature.
  | Land settlement--West (U.S.)--History--19th century--Juvenile
  literature. | Public lands--West (U.S.)--History--19th century--Juvenile
  literature. | West (U.S.)--History--1860-1890--Juvenile literature.
Classification: LCC F596 .H33 2016 | DDC 978/.02--dc23
LC record available at http://lccn.loc.gov/2015048097

Manufactured in Canada

CPSIA Compliance Information: Batch #BS16PK: For further information contact Rosen Publishing, New York, New York at 1-800-237-9932.

CONTENTS

A COUNTRY COAST TO COAST

The United States is one of the largest countries in the world. Covering land from the Atlantic Ocean to the Pacific Ocean, our country takes up the entire width of a continent! But in the earliest days of the United States, only a fraction of this land was occupied.

The original 13 colonies extended from what is now Maine in the Northeast to Georgia in the Southeast. They went inland only as far as New York

This map shows the United States in 1795.

During the 19th century, millions of Americans headed west in search of land and opportunity.

and Pennsylvania. However, west of these boundaries, there were millions of acres of unsettled land.

After the United States became a country, the newly formed government focused on gaining land. Throughout the 1800s, it created policies that encouraged Americans to settle the western **frontier**. This included the **Homestead** Act of 1862, which offered free land to Americans who met certain requirements. This period of westward **expansion** transformed the United States. By the 20th century, the American frontier no longer existed.

THE UNITED STATES GROWS

The idea of westward expansion took off shortly after the United States became a nation. Americans, mostly farmers, began moving west of the Appalachian Mountains into the newly created states of Kentucky and Tennessee. The American economy grew thanks to trade along the Mississippi River and through the southern port city of New Orleans. This territory, however, belonged to France.

The Louisiana Purchase doubled the size of the United States. The territory added under this purchase is highlighted in white.

Meriwether Lewis

William Clark

*After the Louisiana Purchase, Jefferson sent a group called the **Corps** of Discovery to explore the new territory. Led by Meriwether Lewis and William Clark, the Corps of Discovery traveled more than 4,100 miles (6,598 km) between St. Louis and the Pacific Ocean.*

In 1803, the United States purchased 530 million acres (214 million ha) of land from France in a deal known as the Louisiana Purchase. President Thomas Jefferson approved the purchase, which cost $15 million. The United States doubled in size overnight. Now, there was plenty of land to explore and settle.

A few decades after the Louisiana Purchase, an idea called Manifest **Destiny** became popular among many Americans. This was the belief that the United States could—and should—extend from coast to coast.

FACTORS FOR EXPANSION

The idea of Manifest Destiny had been around for years, but it really took hold in the 1840s. During this time, there were many political, social, and economic reasons why the ideas of Manifest Destiny and expansion were popular.

The United States acquired a great amount of land in the 1840s. Thanks to President James K. Polk,

The U.S.-Mexican War ended with the signing of the Treaty of Guadalupe Hidalgo in 1848. Land that was acquired under this treaty later became all or part of the western states of Arizona, California, New Mexico, Colorado, Nevada, and Utah.

This image shows the cover of the Treaty of Guadalupe Hidalgo, which is currently kept in the National Archives in Washington, D.C.

the United States received land from Britain under the Oregon Treaty and land from Mexico after winning the U.S.-Mexican War. Even though much of this territory was taken by force, many Americans supported it because they felt the United States was meant to have it.

Another factor in expansion was the country's growing population. It grew from 5 million in 1800 to 23 million by the 1850s. These people needed somewhere to live. However, there was little land left in the East, where cities, towns, and farms had been growing for decades. In order to own land, many people had to go west.

For many Americans, economic opportunity was the biggest reason for expansion. Owning land was a chance to make money. Many people dreamed of turning unsettled land into farms or businesses that could become a source of income for their family.

After gold was discovered in California in 1848, many fortune-seeking people moved west, hoping to strike it rich. Similar reasons brought **prospectors** to Colorado. Like the waves of **immigrants** who came to America in search of a better life, Americans **migrated** within their own country for the same reasons.

The western frontier also represented other kinds of opportunity. Many Americans felt the West represented change, growth, and freedom. Owning a piece of land was a chance to be **self-sufficient**. For some people, it was a chance to start over. Whatever the reason, the call of the West was answered by people from all over the world.

Western towns grew as people arrived and settled. Cities such as San Francisco, California, and Denver, Colorado, were once **boomtowns**.

THE JOURNEY WEST

Historians estimate about 4 million people moved west between 1820 and 1850. They were called pioneers. Many of them packed their belongings in covered wagons and set out for the unknown. Many pioneers traveled a 2,170-mile (3,492 km) route known as the Oregon Trail.

The journey west was incredibly difficult. The heavy wagons moved very slowly, only covering up

Pioneers traveled in groups called wagon trains. Men, women, and children walked the journey, while teams of oxen pulled the wagons that carried their belongings.

Wagon trains stopped at night so the travelers could rest and prepare for the next day's journey. Here, pioneers gather around a campfire.

to 20 miles (32 km) a day. Pioneers experienced all kinds of weather, including hail, rain, and blazing sun. It was hot during the day and very cold at night. Dust was often so thick it was hard to breathe! Without proper housing, pioneers had no choice but to brave the conditions.

Pioneers had other difficulties, too. Many feared attacks by animals or Native Americans—though most native groups were friendly. Thousands of people died on the trail due to bad conditions and sicknesses. It was common to see gravestones along the trail. However, a new life awaited those who completed the journey.

PIONEER LIFE

The work was not over once pioneers finished their journey. In fact, they faced a whole new set of tasks. They had to clear the land of trees, rocks, and other objects. Then they could plant and build. Growing food was their biggest **priority**. Until settlers could grow their own, they had to eat wild food such as fruit and nuts.

The pioneers had few **resources** in their new

Once at the homestead, oxen were used to clear and plow acres of land.

Many homesteaders built sod homes, such as the one pictured here. Building supplies weren't widely available yet. When railroads arrived in the West, they were able to bring lumber and wood.

land, so they didn't waste anything. They used the trees cleared from the land to build homes and barns. When trees weren't available, they used sod, or earth.

Men, women, and children worked from sunup to sundown. Men and boys cared for the land and their animals. Women and girls cooked, made clothes, and took care of the home. Some pioneers wrote about westward expansion, including author Laura Ingalls Wilder. Her "Little House" series of books taught the world much about pioneer life.

A POLICY OF PREEMPTION

Westward expansion was as important to the U.S. government as it was to individual Americans. Congress had many different policies for how to **distribute** U.S. land. However, few policies lasted long and they were often changed.

Before the 1840s, settlers wanted the government to have a policy called preemption. This was a way to settle and improve land first and pay for it later. Preemption is a form of homesteading.

The Pre-Emption Act was passed in 1841. This allowed people to buy 160 acres (64.7 ha) of land they had already lived on and improved. They could purchase it for at least $1.25 an acre. Many powerful groups opposed this idea. Northern factory owners thought these policies would encourage their workers to leave cities. In the South, people who supported slavery felt preemption would lead to new states that opposed slavery. Congress tried to pass homestead laws three times in the 1850s, but they were blocked each time.

Preemption was sometimes called "Squatters' Rights." Squatters were people who moved onto public land and improved it. However, they didn't legally own it and they faced losing their land—and everything on it—if it was put up for auction. Henry Clay, pictured here, was responsible for the Pre-Emption Act that protected them.

THE HOMESTEAD ACT

Preemption paved the way for the Homestead Act of 1862. Signed by Abraham Lincoln during the Civil War, it's considered to be one of the most important pieces of **legislation** in American history.

The Homestead Act served a few purposes. For many Americans, it was an opportunity to own land and build a future. Lincoln and his government saw it as a chance to populate the West with people who supported Lincoln's pro-**Union**, antislavery causes.

The Homestead Act was advertised as a way to get land—for free! For many Americans, it was an opportunity to build a better life.

The Homestead Act, pictured here, was passed during the American Civil War. It's currently kept in the National Archives in Washington, D.C.

Any citizen or intended citizen who had never "borne arms," or fought against, the United States could become a homesteader. The policy was open to women, immigrants, and, later, African Americans. This was unusual for a time when these groups of people didn't have a lot of rights.

People raced to the West after the Homestead Act passed. Homesteaders received 160 acres (64.7 ha) of land they pledged to live on and improve. They could own the land after five years for a small fee, or they could buy it after six months for $1.25 an acre. The land was sometimes advertised as a "free gift from the government." A popular song told Americans that, "Uncle Sam is rich enough to give us all a farm."

LIFE AS A HOMESTEADER

Daniel Freeman became America's first homesteader on January 1, 1863. He built his homestead near Beatrice, Nebraska. He was one of what became 600,000 Americans who gained land under the Homestead Act through 1900.

Though the promise of free land drew many people to the West, life was not easy for homesteaders. Many left their families behind. They entered an unfamiliar place with few people. Many people told of feeling isolated, or alone, since families lived so far apart. Bad weather and insects damaged crops. Some homesteaders didn't have the means to buy the tools, seeds, and animals needed to build a successful farm. In many cases, conditions were so tough that homesteaders left their land before five years.

Life became easier for homesteaders who stuck it out. Railroads arrived in the West in the late 1860s. Their arrival brought great change. It became easier for people and supplies to travel to the West and back.

first homestead

Congress recognized Daniel Freeman as the first homesteader in 1936. Today, a national monument stands in Beatrice, Nebraska. The monument honors the important role homesteaders like Freeman had in growing and shaping the United States.

TRANSFORMING A NATION

More than 270 million acres (109 million ha) of land were distributed under the Homestead Act. That's about 10 percent of all U.S. land! However, most of the land went to railroads, cattlemen, miners, and lumbermen. Some of it went to land **speculators**.

The Homestead Act transformed the United States in many ways. Frontier towns grew as homesteaders arrived. Schools, churches, and towns became the center of frontier life. Soon, western territories became states, and the country continued to grow.

The Great Plains region became a center of agriculture. Ranching became an important industry, too. In 1860, there were 130,000 cattle in the Plains states. By 1880, that number rose to 4.5 million!

The Homestead Act lasted until 1976—long after homesteaders tamed the western frontier. Today, westward expansion is seen as one of the most important periods in American history.

GLOSSARY

boomtown (BOOM-town): A town that grows quickly because of something important, such as the discovery of gold, that happens nearby.

corps (KOHR): A group of people assigned to a particular kind of work.

destiny (DEH-stuh-nee): Events that are meant to happen to someone or something in the future.

distribute (dih-STRIH-byoot): To give out.

expansion (ihk-SPAN-shun): The action of becoming larger or more spread out.

frontier (fruhn-TEER): The wilderness that lies at the edge of settled territory.

homestead (HOHM-sted): In the 19th and 20th centuries, an area of land given to U.S. citizens to settle and improve.

immigrant (IH-muh-grunt): A person who comes to live permanently in another country.

legislation (leh-juh-SLAY-shun): Laws.

migrate (MY-grayt): To move from one area to settle in another.

priority (pry-OHR-ih-tee): Something that is considered more important than other things.

prospector (PRAH-spehk-tohr): A person who travels to an area to look for gold or other valuable minerals.

resource (REE-sohrz): Something in nature that can be used by people.

self-sufficient (SELF–suh-FIH-shunt): Needing no outside help.

speculator (SPEH-kyoo-lay-tuhr): In the 19th century, a person who buys a large amount of land in the hopes of making money in the future.

Union (YOON-yuhn): The Northern states during the American Civil War; also, a name for the United States as a whole.

23

INDEX

PRIMARY SOURCE LIST

Page 8: *Battle of Churubusco*. Created by John Cameron and published by Nathaniel Currier. Hand-colored lithograph. ca. 1846. Now kept at the Library of Congress Prints and Photographs Division, Washington, D.C.

Page 9: The Treaty of Guadalupe Hidalgo (Exchange Copy). Created by the governments of the United States and Mexico. Ink on paper. February 2, 1848. Now kept at the National Archives and Records Administration, Washington, D.C.

Page 19: The Homestead Act. Created by the United States Congress. Ink on paper. May 20, 1862. Now kept at the National Archives and Records Administration, Washington, D.C.

Page 20: The first homestead. Created by A.R. Campbell. Photograph. ca. 1887. Now kept at the Library of Congress Prints and Photographs Division, Washington, D.C.

WEBSITES

Due to the changing nature of Internet links, PowerKids Press has developed an online list of websites related to the subject of this book. This site is updated regularly. Please use this link to access the list: www.powerkidslinks.com/soah/west